HARDWOOD GREATS

PRO BASKETBALL'S BEST PLAYERS

PAUL GEORGE

HARDWOOD GREATS

PRO BASKETBALL'S BEST PLAYERS

CHRIS PAUL

GIANNIS ANTETOKOUNMPO

JAMES HARDEN

KEVIN DURANT

LEBRON JAMES

PAUL GEORGE

RUSSELL WESTBROOK

STEPHEN CURRY

HARDWOOD GREATS

PRO BASKETBALL'S BEST PLAYERS

PAUL GEORGE

DONALD PARKER

MASON CREST

PHILADELPHIA

MIAMI

Mason Crest
450 Parkway Drive, Suite D
Broomall, Pennsylvania 19008
(866) MCP-BOOK (toll-free)
www.masoncrest.com

First printing
9 8 7 6 5 4 3 2 1

ISBN (hardback) 978-1-4222-4350-3
ISBN (series) 978-1-4222- 4344-2
ISBN (ebook) 978-1-4222- 7465-1

Cataloging-in-Publication Data on file with the Library of Congress

Developed and Produced by National Highlights Inc.
Editor: Andrew Luke
Interior and cover design: Annalisa Gumbrecht, Studio Gumbrecht
Production: Michelle Luke

QR CODES AND LINKS TO THIRD-PARTY CONTENT

CONTENTS

KEY ICONS TO LOOK FOR:

Words to Understand: These words with their easy-to-understand definitions will increase the reader's understanding of the text while building vocabulary skills.

Sidebars: This boxed material within the main text allows readers to build knowledge, gain insights, explore possibilities, and broaden their perspectives by weaving together additional information to provide realistic and holistic perspectives.

Educational Videos: Readers can view videos by scanning our QR codes, providing them with additional educational content to supplement the text. Examples include news coverage, moments in history, speeches, iconic sports moments, and much more!

Text-Dependent Questions: These questions send the reader back to the text for more careful attention to the evidence presented there.

Research Projects: Readers are pointed toward areas of further inquiry connected to each chapter. Suggestions are provided for projects that encourage deeper research and analysis.

Series Glossary of Key Terms: This back-of-the-book glossary contains terminology used throughout this series. Words found here increase the reader's ability to read and comprehend higher-level books and articles in this field.

WORDS TO UNDERSTAND

milestone: A significant event or stage in the life, progress, development (or the like) of a person, nation, etc.

plateau: A level of attainment or achievement

strike: A work stoppage by a body of workers to enforce compliance with demands made on an employer

truncated: Shortened as if by having a part cut off; cut short

CHAPTER 1

GREATEST MOMENTS

PAUL GEORGE'S NBA CAREER

Paul George had to come a long way in his career to be considered one of the best in the league. He is six feet nine inches (2.06 m) tall, weighs 220 pounds (100 kg), and can play both small forward and shooting guard. George has helped lead both the Indiana Pacers of the Eastern Conference and the Oklahoma City Thunder of the Western Conference to multiple playoff appearances. This includes consecutive conference finals appearances as part of playoff appearances in each of his first nine seasons, except for the 2014–2015 (which was **truncated** by a serious leg injury).

The Indiana Pacers selected George with the 10th pick of the 2010 NBA (National Basketball Association) draft, which is where he was projected to

George became a star in Indiana, where he played his first seven seasons with the Pacers.

be taken. George rewarded the team's faith in him by earning his way into the starting lineup (he started a total of 19 games in 2010–2011 and played in 61) and added 476 points, 62 steals, and 224 total rebounds.

George was named to the NBA's All-Rookie second team. His successful rookie year served as a foundation for him to build on as he turned himself into a premier player in the NBA. After being traded to Oklahoma City in 2017, George paired with point guard Russell Westbrook to become master ball thieves—displaying a talent they both share for stealing the basketball from their opponents. He joined the 10,000 career points club during the 2018–2019 season and has established himself as a force on both the offensive and defensive sides of the ball.

George's ability to steal the ball makes him a lethal defender on the floor, and he is considered one of the best two-way players in the NBA. George is respected not only for his three-point shooting ability and unselfish play on the offensive side of the basketball, but also for his defensive skill and the pure athleticism he brings every night to the floor.

George was not highly sought after as a high school player. He did play for a few Amateur Athletic Union (AAU) teams, however, and managed to raise his profile enough to receive a recruiting offer from California State University at Fresno, also referred to as Fresno State (nickname: "Bulldogs"). Two years of college basketball were enough for NBA scouts to notice him and give him an opportunity to play at the professional level.

George was an important piece to Indiana's winning formula, helping lead the team to the playoffs in all but one of his seven seasons. He helped the Thunder make the playoffs in both seasons in Oklahoma, and his addition to the LA Clippers team in 2019 has raised its prospects for the future!

PAUL GEORGE'S GREATEST CAREER MOMENTS

HERE IS A LIST OF

SOME OF THE CAREER

FIRSTS AND GREATEST

ACHIEVEMENTS DURING

HIS TIME IN THE NBA:

George led Indiana to the playoffs in six of his seven seasons with the Pacers.

10,000 POINTS SCORED IN A CAREER

George reached the 10,000 career points scored **milestone** in the 2018–2019 NBA season. On November 2, 2018, during a game against fellow 2010 NBA draft pick John Wall (number one overall) of the Washington Wizards, George put up 17 points to go along with seven assists and four rebounds. His effort was more than enough to lead the Oklahoma City Thunder to a 134–111 victory. The 17 points that he notched in the game put him over the 10,000 points scored mark for his NBA career.

A November 2, 2018, victory over the Wizards saw George contribute 17 points in the game and reach the 10,000 points **plateau** in career scoring.

41 POINTS SCORED IN THE ALL-STAR GAME

George was named a starter for the Eastern Conference All-Star team in the 2015–2016 season as a member of the Indiana Pacers. Playing alongside LeBron James, Dwyane Wade, Carmelo Anthony, and former 2010 number-one draft selection John Wall of the Washington Wizards, George scored a game-high 41 points. Although the East All-Stars came up short against the West in a 196–173 loss, the 41 points were the highest point total he has had in any of his All-Star appearances.

George puts up a 41-point total in a February 14, 2016, All-Star appearance at the Air Canada Centre in Toronto, Ontario (Canada).

3

FIRST CAREER TRIPLE-DOUBLE

In the 2012–2013 season George recorded his first career triple-double in points, assists, and total rebounds. On February 13, 2013, in a game against the Charlotte Bobcats, George put up 23 points (leading all scorers in the game), grabbed 12 rebounds, including 11 on the defensive boards, and dished out 12 assists in nearly 39 minutes of play. His efforts led the Pacers to a dominant 101–77 blowout victory over the Bobcats.

George scored 23 points and contributed heavily to the Pacers' win over the Bobcats in a February 2013 game that marked his first NBA career triple-double.

NAMED TO 2017 NBA ALL-DEFENSIVE SECOND TEAM

George received tremendous recognition for his defensive skills when he was named to the NBA's All-Defensive second team in 2013. He was also named to the All-NBA third team that season. The All-Defensive team honors, given since the 1968–1969 NBA season, go to the 10 best defensive players in the league, divided into the first and second teams. For that season, he finished in the top 20 in steals (sixth with 143) and defensive rebounds (15th with 515). He has since made the All-Defensive first team twice (2014, 2019), and was again be named to the NBA All-Defensive second team in 2016.

Highlights of George in the 2012–2013 NBA season doing what he does best—blocking shots, grabbing defensive boards, and accumulating ball steals, all of which led to his first All-Defensive team selection.

FORTY-EIGHT POINTS SCORED IN A GAME

George had scored 40 points or more in a game a few times in his career prior to the December 5, 2015, matchup against the Utah Jazz. In the game, in which his Indiana Pacers lost by the score of 122–119, he dropped 48 points, pulled down eight rebounds, and dished out three assists to go with three steals. The 48 points scored were the most that he has ever scored in a game in his NBA career.

Highlights showing George scoring 48 points in a close loss to the Utah Jazz in December 2015.

NAMED NBA MOST IMPROVED PLAYER

George came out of his second season with the Indiana Pacers averaging 12.1 points per game with 798 points scored in the **strike**-shortened 2011–2012 campaign. His performance was slightly better than his rookie season, but as a member of the NBA's All-Rookie second team, expectations were higher for his sophomore season. It was in George's third season that he stepped up to show why he was a top-10 draft selection. He increased his scoring to an average of 17.4 points per game and took over as leader of the Indiana team, which finished the season with a 49–32 record, a Central Division title, and a number-three seeding in the 2013 playoffs. George was voted the NBA Most Improved Player for the 2012–2013 season.

Becoming a consistent player helped George improve his game in 2013 and earn honors as the league's Most Improved Player.

NAMED TO FIRST NBA ALL-STAR TEAM (2013)

George had a breakout 2012–2013 season for the Indiana Pacers. He finished in the top 20 in the league in several offensive and defensive categories, including steals, rebounds, and three-point field goals made. The improvement from his previous season (2011–2012) to 2013, showed that George was worthy of a top-10, first-round pick. He was rewarded for his successful turnaround in the 2013 season with a selection to that season's All-Star game as a reserve for the Eastern Conference. For that game, George scored 17 points to lead all reserves, including 3-for-6 shooting from the three-point line in a 143–138 loss to the Western All-Stars.

George proves that he is a top-level NBA player with a 17-point effort in the 2013 NBA All-Star game on February 17, 2013, at the Toyota Center in Houston, Texas.

8

LED EASTERN CONFERENCE NBA PLAYOFFS IN STEALS (2014)

Besides leading the 2014 playoffs in three-point shooting, George also showed his defensive skills—which is why he has been named to the NBA All-Defensive squad in three separate seasons. His 41 steals in the 19 games he played (through game 6 of the Eastern Conference Finals) tied him with Oklahoma City Thunder (and future teammate) Russell Westbrook of the Western Conference for most in the playoffs. This helped establish George as not only an improved player but also one to watch out for in the coming years.

George's 37-point effort in game 5 of the 2014 Eastern Conference Finals against the LeBron James–led Miami Heat included six of the 41 steals he totaled in the playoffs.

Oklahoma City traded for George before the 2017 season despite his expiring contract. He enjoyed the year in Oklahoma playing with Russell Westbrook enough to sign a new four-year deal with the Thunder in 2018. The Thunder then traded George to the LA Clippers in 2019.

TEXT-DEPENDENT QUESTIONS

1. On what date and against what team did George score his 10,000th career point? How many points did he score in the game?

2. When did he record his first career triple-double? Who was his opponent?

3. What conference (East or West) did he represent when he scored 41 points in the 2016 NBA All-Star game?

 RESEARCH PROJECT

The Most Improved Player (MIP) award is an honor that has been given to players in the NBA since 1986. It is awarded to the player who has shown the most improvement between seasons. There are several players besides George who played in the 2018–2019 season that won the MIP and were also named to the All-Star team in the same season. Do some research to determine who these players are, the team they play for, and the number of honors they have received since being named MIP.

WORDS TO UNDERSTAND

budding: At an early stage of development but showing promise or potential

subsequent: Occurring or coming later or after

varsity: Any first-string team, especially in sports, that represents a school, college, university, or the like

CHAPTER 2

THE ROAD TO THE TOP
GEORGE'S PLAYER PERFORMANCE

Paul Clifton Anthony George was born in Palmdale, California, on May 2, 1990. His parents, Paul and Paulette George, raised him with two older sisters. His sister, Teiosha, was a basketball player for the Pepperdine University "Wave" women's basketball team (as a forward); his other sister, Portala, was a volleyball player for the California State University at San Bernardino "Coyotes." Portala's six feet 1 inch (1.85 m) height, and Teiosha's six feet four inch (1.93 m) frame suggest that the George children were destined to be athletic siblings!

George attended Knight High School (nickname: "Hawks") in Palmdale but did not make the **varsity** team until the start of his sophomore year at the school. Participation on a local AAU team between his junior and senior years

George chose to play college basketball at Fresno State University over bigger programs at Georgetown and Penn State.

and elevating his role with the Hawks in his senior year helped raise his profile with college scouts. George averaged 23.2 points per game and 11.2 rebounds as a senior, and his performance was good enough to consider scholarship offers from several schools including Santa Clara University (nickname: "Broncos"), Pepperdine (nickname: "Waves"), Georgetown University (nickname: "Hoyas"), and Penn State University (nickname: '"Nittany Lions'). He ultimately chose another offer to attend Fresno State.

George spent two years playing for the Bulldogs. During his years in college, George led the team in steals and rebounds in both his freshman and sophomore years. In his first year, he was second in scoring on the Bulldogs' team with 487 points scored for an average of 14.3 points per game. George led Fresno State in his sophomore season (2009–2010) in scoring with an average of 16.8 points per game and another 487 points scored. These numbers were enough to convince NBA scouts that he was a prospective player with a huge potential for success.

George chose not to return to school for his junior year and entered the NBA draft. Indiana used the 10th pick to select him. George's first nine seasons in the NBA, with both the Pacers and Oklahoma City, saw him chosen for the NBA All-Star game in six of those seasons. He was a member of the All-Rookie (second) team and received the award for most improved player in the 2012–2013

George played for his country at the 2016 Olympic Games in Rio de Janeiro, Brazil.

season. His fast hands make him one of the best ball thieves in the game, and he has been in the top 10 for steals in five of his nine seasons. An injury during an exhibition game for Team USA kept him from playing in the 2014 FIBA (*Fedération Internationale de Basket-Ball*) World Cup game in Barcelona, Spain, but he did receive the Olympic Gold in 2016 as a member of the U.S. Men's National Basketball Team and their triumph in Rio de Janeiro.

NBA DRAFT DAY 2010 SIGNIFICANT ACCOUNTS

- Paul George was selected by the Indiana Pacers with the 10th pick in the first round of the 2010 NBA draft.

- The 2010 NBA draft was held at Madison Square Garden in New York City on June 24, 2010. This would be the last draft conducted at Madison Square Garden; in **subsequent** years the draft was moved first to the Prudential Center (Newark, New Jersey) in 2011 and 2012, and then to the Barclays Center in Brooklyn, New York, from 2013–2018.

- George was the eighth of eight forwards selected with the first 10 picks of the 2010 NBA draft.

- He was one of 32 forwards (23 power forwards and nine small forwards) taken in the 2010 NBA draft (out of the 60 players drafted in rounds 1 and 2).

- Harvard University senior point guard Jeremy Lin entered the 2010 draft, but was not selected. Lin would go on to start for six NBA teams and play nearly 500 career games.

- The forward position was the largest group drafted in the 2010 draft, followed by guards (19), and centers (nine).

- Five players from the University of Kentucky Wildcat's 2009–2010 Elite Eight squad were all drafted in the first round of the 2010 NBA draft: John Wall (first pick); DeMarcus Cousins (fifth pick); Patrick Patterson (14th pick); Eric Bledsoe (18th pick); and Daniel Orton (29th pick).

- Nine players chosen in the 2010 NBA draft have never played a single NBA game, with the highest pick of these being Terrico White of the University of Mississippi picked 36th overall by Detroit.

- The Washington Wizards won the right to the first pick by winning the NBA draft lottery. The Wizards had the fifth-worst record, but prevailed in the lottery despite just a 10 percent chance to win.

Source: https://stats.nba.com/draft/history/?Season=2010—NBA draft information for 2010 NBA draft.

In high school, George was an AAU teammate of current NBA guard Jrue Holiday.

ATHLETIC ACCOMPLISHMENTS IN HIGH SCHOOL AND COLLEGE

HIGH SCHOOL

George attended high school beginning in 2004 at Knight High School in his hometown of Palmdale, California. Palmdale is a city located in the central part of Los Angeles County, that is 63 miles north of the city of Los Angeles (on the other side of the San Gabriel Mountains in what is known as "Antelope Valley"). He played on the junior varsity team during his freshman year and it wasn't until the following year that he made varsity.

George appeared in 21 games, scoring 114 points and averaging 5.4 points a game. He saw limited time in his junior year, appearing in only nine games, but raised his scoring average to 13.9 points a game. After working on his game by playing on a local AAU squad with future NBA star Jrue Holiday of the New Orleans Pelicans, his coach increased George's playing time in his senior year. That boost was what he needed to get the attention of college recruiters.

Although his 23.2 scoring average and 11.1 rebounds a game helped lead his Hawks team to a Golden Valley championship in 2008, George was only considered a three-star recruit by Rivals.com, far below many of his local rivals. Holiday, who was 50 miles to the west in Chatsworth, California, was the 2008 Gatorade National Player of the Year and considered the number-one point guard in the country. Fellow Californian DeMar DeRozan (San Antonio Spurs) from Compton (Los Angeles) was also a McDonald's All-American and

Parade Magazine First Team All-American with Holiday. George did not receive consideration for any of the high school All-American squads in 2008.

Here are George's three-year statistics from his time at Knight High School in Palmdale:

Season/Yr	G	FGM	FG%	FTM	FT%	TRB	AST	STL	BLK	PTS	PPG	RPG	AST
2005–06/ Sophomore	21	43	38.0%	14	66.7%	64	12	20	13	114	5.4	3.0	0.6
2006–07/ Junior	9	50	49.0%	15	65.2%	59	17	18	12	125	13.9	6.6	1.9
2007–08/ Senior	23	188	48.0%	97	75.2%	256	66	71	39	533	23.2	11.1	2.9
TOTALS	53	281	46.0%	126	72.8%	379	95	109	64	772	14.6	7.2	1.8

COLLEGE

George sparked the interest of several schools in his area such as Pepperdine (where his sister attended five years earlier as a forward on the women's basketball team), Santa Clara, Fresno State, and two out-of-state schools: Georgetown and Penn State of the Big Ten Conference.

George initially gave a verbal commitment to Santa Clara but withdrew and decided instead to go Pepperdine University to follow in the footsteps of his older sibling. He then chose not to go to Pepperdine when the coach that recruited him left the program before he stepped on campus. George made a final decision to accept an offer to play at Fresno State University.

George played his college home games at Fresno State's Save Mart Center.

George saw improvement in his game from his freshman to sophomore years in college. His scoring average went from 14.3 points a game to 16.8 points per game. George's defensive stats remained fairly consistent (steal, blocks, rebounds), and he scored the same number of points in 2008 as he did in 2009:

Season	G	FGM	FG%	FTM	FT%	TRB	AST	STL	BLK	PTS	PPG	RPG	AST
2008–09	34	166	47.0%	92	69.7%	212	63	59	34	487	14.3	6.2	1.9
2009–10	29	154	42.4%	120	90.9%	210	88	64	24	487	16.8	7.2	3.0
TOTALS	63	320	44.7%	212	80.3%	422	151	123	58	974	15.5	6.7	2.4

TALENT RUNS DEEP IN THE GEORGE HOUSEHOLD

Paul George has a nice NBA contract, but he is not the only gifted sibling in the George family. He is the only son of Paul and Paulette George's three children; their two older daughters also made their marks in collegiate sports. George's sister Teiosha was a forward on the Pepperdine University Wave women's basketball team, appearing in the women's NCAA (National Collegiate Athletic Association) Championship tournament in 2003 and women's NIT (National Invitation Tournament) tournament in 2004—two more post-season tournaments than her brother had at Fresno State. These days she has turned her attention to the music industry.

George's older sister Teiosha hung up her basketball shoes and exchanged them for a microphone and a chance at a career as a **budding** recording artist.

At the end of his sophomore season, George made the decision to declare for the NBA draft.

GEORGE, DEMAR DEROZAN, AND JRUE HOLIDAY

George ranked 20th out of high school prospects in a class that included future NBA stars DeMar DeRozan (San Antonio Spurs) and Jrue Holiday (New Orleans Pelicans). Coming out of high school, Holiday and DeRozan received more praise and honors than George. While George ended up playing at Fresno State for two years, Holiday was recruited by the University of California at Los Angeles (UCLA, nickname: "Bruins") while DeRozan went across town from Holiday to attend the University of Southern California (USC, nickname: "Trojans").

DeRozan declared for the 2009 NBA draft and was the ninth selection overall by the Toronto Raptors. Holiday was also drafted in 2009 by the Philadelphia 76ers with the 17th pick. Between these three players they have been named to a total of 11 All-Star games (George: six; DeRozan: four, Holiday: one), six All-Pro squads (George: four; DeRozan: two), four All-Defensive teams (George: three; Holiday: one), one All-Rookie (George), and one Most Improved Player (George).

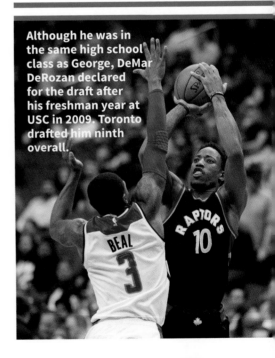

Although he was in the same high school class as George, DeMar DeRozan declared for the draft after his freshman year at USC in 2009. Toronto drafted him ninth overall.

Holiday averaged almost four assists a game in his rookie season with Philadelphia.

Here is a look at the three Californians' first year totals in the NBA:

ROOKIE SEASON

Season	Player	Tm	G	FG%	REB	AST	STL	BLK	PTS	PPG	RPG	APG
2009–10	DeRozan	Toronto	77	49.8%	223	53	43	18	662	8.6	2.9	0.7
2009–10	Holiday	Philadelphia	73	44.2%	191	280	79	18	587	8.0	2.6	3.8
2010–11	*George*	*Indiana*	*61*	*45.3%*	*224*	*65*	*62*	*26*	*476*	*7.8*	*3.7*	*1.1*

DeRozan shot nearly 50 percent from the field as a rookie for the Raptors.

TEXT-DEPENDENT QUESTIONS

1. What high school did George attend? In what city is the school located?

2. What team drafted George in the 2010 NBA draft? What number draft pick was used to select him?

3. What college did he choose to attend? What year did he start playing college basketball? How many years did he attend college?

 # RESEARCH PROJECT

George comes from an athletic family. Both his sisters played major college sports. He is not the only player who has athletic sisters. Looking a 20-year span of the NBA draft (1999–2018), identify at least five top-10 NBA draft selections whose sisters also excelled in college and/or women's professional sports. Name the player, the player's sister's name, the college she attended, and the sport in which she participated.

WORDS TO UNDERSTAND

exhibition: A sporting event whose outcome has no impact on the ranking or standings of players or teams

mock: To mimic, imitate, or counterfeit

prospect: A likely candidate for a job or position

CHAPTER 3

ON THE COURT
PRE-DRAFT ASSESSMENT

After two season of college basketball, George was ready to see if his talent was enough to carry him on to the next level. NBA scouts rated him a 95 out of a possible score of 100 as a potential pro, which led to teams giving him high consideration in the 2010 draft. George was projected to be a number-10 pick based on NBA analyst big boards and **mock** drafts. At the position of small forward, he was rated the third best in the draft.

After George's performance in the NBA's pre-draft camp that was held in Chicago in May of 2010 (just prior to the 2010 NBA draft), scouts and analysts around the league felt that he was a defensive asset that would bring value to a team willing to consider him in the first round. He possessed the size, athleticism, and skills to be a more-than-adequate scorer and a player with good-to-great potential.

George made an impact in Indiana right away, getting named to the NBA All-Rookie team in his first season.

A rookie season that saw George score 476 points for a 7.8 points per game average, commit 62 steals, and grab 224 rebounds (including 187 defensive rebounds) was good enough to land him on the All-Rookie team. Assessments of his potential as an NBA **prospect** were fairly precise when looking at his performance over his first nine seasons. George has won various awards, honors, and recognition for his play and also secured a large contract from the Oklahoma City Thunder to continue in the league through at least the end of the 2022 season. He was traded to the LA Clippers one year into his new deal.

Also, since coming to the league, George has been recognized as follows:

- Named NBA Player of the Week, eight times:
    - ➜ December 16, 2012
    - ➜ November 11, 2013
    - ➜ January 20, 2014
    - ➜ November 30, 2015
    - ➜ April 10, 2017
    - ➜ December 24, 2018
    - ➜ January 28, 2019
    - ➜ February 11, 2019

- Named NBA Player of the Month, three times:
    - ➜ November 2013
    - ➜ November 2015
    - ➜ April 2017

George watches as teammate Steven Adams chases a loose ball in a 2019 game against Miami.

ON-THE-COURT ACCOMPLISHMENTS

George has managed to meet and exceed expectations since joining the league. He is a member of the 10,000-points-scored-in-a-career club, achieved in a November 2, 2018, matchup against the Washington Wizards. He helped restore the Indiana Pacers to contender status, leading them to back-to-back NBA Eastern Conference Finals in 2013 and 2014. George played alongside Russell Westbrook in Oklahoma City through the 2018-2019 season, and will now play with Kawhi Leonard to help a Clippers franchise that made the playoffs eight of the previous nine seasons take the next step.

PAUL GEORGE

GUARD/FORWARD

- Date of birth: May 2, 1990

- Height: Six feet nine inches (2.06 m), Weight: Approx. 220 pounds (99 kg)

- Drafted in the first round in 2010 (10th pick overall) by the Indiana Pacers

- College: California State University at Fresno (nickname: "Bulldogs")

- Two-time NBA All-Defensive First Team (2014, 2019)

- Two-time NBA All-Defensive Second team (2013, 2016)

- Six-time NBA All-Star (2013, 2014, 2016–2019)

- All-NBA First Team (2019)

- NBA Most Improved Player (2013)

- NBA steals leader with 170 (2.2 per game) in 2019

CAREER TOTALS

Here are the career, playoff, and All-Star game numbers George has put up through the 2018–2019 NBA season:

Regular Season Career Totals

SEASON	TM	G	FGM	FG%	FTM	FT%	REB	AST	STL	BLK	PTS	PPG
2010–11	IND	61	179	45.3%	77	76.2%	224	65	62	26	476	7.8
2011–12	IND	66	281	44.0%	146	80.2%	370	158	108	38	798	12.1
2012–13	IND	79	493	41.9%	221	80.7%	603	327	143	51	1377	17.4
2013–14	IND	80	577	42.4%	401	86.4%	542	283	151	22	1737	21.7
2014–15	IND	6	18	36.7%	8	72.7%	22	6	5	1	53	8.8
2015–16	IND	81	605	41.8%	454	86.0%	563	329	152	29	1874	23.1
2016–17	IND	75	622	46.1%	336	89.8%	492	251	119	27	1775	23.7
2017–18	OKC	79	576	43.0%	338	82.2%	447	263	161	39	1734	21.9
2018–19	OKC	77	707	43.8%	453	83.9%	628	318	170	34	2159	28.0
TOTAL		**604**	**4,058**	**43.3%**	**2,434**	**84.4%**	**3,891**	**2,000**	**1,071**	**267**	**11,983**	**19.8**

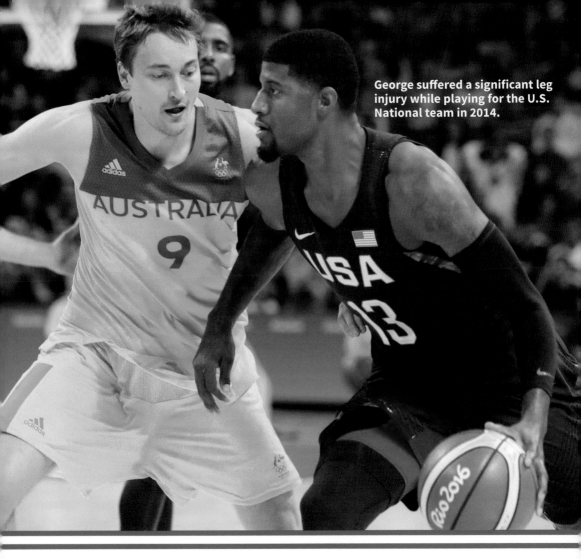

George suffered a significant leg injury while playing for the U.S. National team in 2014.

While playing in an **exhibition** game as a member of the U.S. Men's National team in 2014 (in preparation for the 2014 FIBA Basketball World Cup tournament in Barcelona, Spain), George injured himself while guarding Houston Rockets superstar James Harden. The leg injury that he sustained as a result kept him out of all but the last six games of the 2014–2015 season.

PLAYOFF TOTALS

George has appeared in a total of 71 playoff games in his career with both Indiana and Oklahoma City. He has scored a total of 1,382 points in these appearances for a per-game average of 19.5 points. During the 2013–2014 playoff run, George led his team in points scored (429), steals (41), defensive (132) and total rebounds (141), free throw shooting (101 free throws made of 128 for a 78.9 percent shooting percentage), three-point shooting (52 free throws made of 129 for a 40.3 percent shooting percentage), and field goals made and attempted (138 of 315). The George-led Pacers team fell to eventual NBA champions, Miami Heat, losing the series four games to two. The "Big Three" of LeBron James, Dwyane Wade, and Chris Bosh led the Heat.

George and the Pacers were not able to overcome the Big Three from eventual champions Miami in the 2014 playoffs.

Here are George's performance statistics for his 76 playoff games:

SEASON	TM	G	FGM	FG%	FTM	FT%	REB	AST	STL	BLK	PTS	PPG
2010–11	IND	5	10	30.3%	7	87.5%	25	5	7	10	30	6.0
2011–12	IND	11	37	38.9%	22	78.6%	73	26	18	4	107	9.7
2012–13	IND	19	119	43.0%	93	72.7%	141	96	25	9	365	19.2
2013–14	IND	19	138	43.8%	101	78.9%	145	73	41	7	429	22.6
2015–16	IND	7	56	45.5%	61	95.3%	53	30	14	5	191	27.3
2016–17	IND	4	34	38.6%	26	86.7%	35	29	7	2	112	28.0
2017–18	OKC	6	49	40.8%	31	86.1%	36	16	8	4	148	24.7
2018-19	OKC	5	44	43.6%	40	81.6	43	18	7	1	143	28.6
TOTAL		76	487	42.3%	381	80.9%	551	293	127	42	1,525	20.1

ALL-STAR GAMES TOTALS

George has played in six All-Star games (2013, 2014, 2016–2019). He was named a starter in three of the six games (2014, 2016, and 2019) and has averaged 20.8 points per game (not including his 2019 performance). George led all All-Star scorers in the 2016 game with 41 points, in a 196–173 loss to the West All-Stars. Here are his All-Star game scoring totals (through 2019):

SEASON	TM	GS	FGM	FG%	REB	AST	STL	BLK	PTS	PPG
2012–13	IND	0	7	53.8%	3	4	2	0	17	17.0
2013–14	IND	1	6	46.2%	5	5	2	0	18	18.0
2015–16	IND	1	16	61.5%	5	1	1	0	41	41.0
2016–17	IND	0	6	37.5%	5	3	0	0	12	12.0
2017–18	OKC	0	6	40.0%	5	4	1	0	16	16.0
2018–19	OKC	1	7	50.0%	2	4	3	0	20	20
TOTAL		6	48	49.5%	25	21	9	0	124	20.7

 # DESTINED FOR GREATNESS

Many teams had George rising up their chart in mock draft scenarios as their scouts speculated as to whether the kid from Fresno State was the "real deal." George, prior to entering the 2010 draft, did not face the strongest competition in college, but impressed when working out for the teams interested in drafting him. Interestingly, of the eight forwards selected in the first round in 2010 (five power forwards and three small forwards including George), he was the last one selected. Compared to the two small forwards taken ahead of him (Evan Turner, second pick to Philadelphia, and Wesley Johnson, fourth pick to Minnesota), George has by far had the most successful career in nine seasons (in terms of scoring and honors).

George appears on Minnesota Timberwolves TV discussing the reasons for his sudden rise as a potential NBA star. Although the Timberwolves were interested in George, they chose Wesley Johnson, a small forward from Syracuse University who spent just two seasons in Minnesota.

DeMarcus Cousins, chosen fifth overall out of Kentucky, is the only player from the draft class to score more points than George in the NBA by the end of the 2019 season.

RANKING GEORGE

George's career compares favorably with that of the other top-10 picks in the 2010 draft:

Pk	Player	Draft Team	2018-19 Team	Yrs	G	PTS	REB	AST	PPG
5	DeMarcus Cousins	Kings	Warriors	9	565	12006	6131	1832	21.2
10	*Paul George*	*Pacers*	*Thunder*	*9*	*604*	*11983*	*3891*	*2000*	*19.8*
1	John Wall	Wizards	Wizards	9	573	10879	2483	5282	19.0
9	Gordon Hayward	Jazz	Celtics	9	589	8904	2472	2006	15.1
7	Greg Monroe	Pistons	Raptors	9	632	8326	5229	1354	13.2
3	Derrick Favors	Nets	Jazz	9	632	7320	4547	701	11.6
2	Evan Turner	76ers	Blazers	9	686	6762	3240	2424	9.9
8	Al-Farouq Aminu	Clippers	Blazers	9	670	5170	4083	827	7.7
4	Wesley Johnson	T'Wolves	Wizards	9	609	4235	1924	645	7.0
6	Ekpe Udoh*	Warriors	Jazz	7	384	1353	1100	260	3.5

*Udoh played in the EuroLeague for Istanbul-Turkey (Fenerbahce SK Basketball) for the 2015–2016 and 2016–2017 NBA seasons.

George has certainly established himself in the NBA. His body of work shows that nine teams should have had second thoughts about passing him over in the 2010 NBA draft. He has developed into a top player, a three-point shooting threat, a defensive star, and a player who makes his teams better on both ends of the floor.

George has had a career at least on par if not better than that of the Wizards' John Wall, who was the first overall pick in George's draft year.

TEXT-DEPENDENT QUESTIONS

1. How many points has George scored in his career through the first 581 games played? What is his average points scored per game?

2. How many All-Star games has he participated in? How many All-Star games has he started in his career?

3. What other player was involved in George's 2014 injury? What event was he preparing for when he was injured?

RESEARCH PROJECT

Tenth overall can be a good position in which to be drafted. For George, it has led to appearances in two Eastern Conference Finals, six All-Star games, four All-NBA teams, three All-Defensive teams, and a Most Improved Player award. Looking at the players who were selected with the 10th pick in the NBA draft from 2009–2018, determine how many played in the NBA during the 2018–2019 season. Also determine who (if any) were named to an All-Star team, All-NBA team, All-Defensive or Offensive team, or have won any award such as Most Improved or Most Valuable Player.

WORDS TO UNDERSTAND

cerebral: Involving intelligence rather than emotions or instinct

literacy: The quality or state of being able to read and write

prejudice: An unfavorable opinion or feeling formed beforehand or without knowledge, thought, or reason

proponent: A person who argues in favor of something; an advocate

stereotype: Simplified and standardized conception or image invested with special meaning and held in common by members of a group

CHAPTER 4

WORDS COUNT

When the time comes to address the media before or after a game, players either retreat to the comfort of traditional phrases that avoid controversy (Cliché City), or they speak their mind with refreshing candor (Quote Machine).

Here are 10 quotes, compiled in part from the azquotes.com website, with some insight as to the context of what George is talking about or referencing:

> "We don't give (people) a gun without training them. We don't give them a car without training them. Why would we give them a computer without the appropriate training?"

George has worked to get technology training for underprivileged children.

George has been the beneficiary of great success as a result of his play on the basketball court. He is a huge **proponent** of giving back to the community and likes to involve himself in charitable activities. He is especially proud of the work he has done for children from low-income or disadvantaged backgrounds. He is passionate about education and helping students gain access to the resources that they need to be competitive in a world that requires **literacy** in many different areas, not just reading. With this quote, George challenges others to not only provide new computers or other types of technology to students, but to also provide them with the necessary training to gain the skills they need in life. **Rating: Quote Machine**

> **"Every other time this issue has been looked at people have shied away from doing anything further because it's too easy to say nothing can be done."**

The issue George is referring to is that of the **prejudice** that some people have toward youth, particularly African American youth that come from poorer communities. This prejudice, as he sees it, clouds people's judgment of the potential that these youths have and prevents them from doing more to help improve their lives. George takes a **cerebral** approach to issues like this, asking why more can't be done to help. His life is an example of overcoming difficult circumstances, in which instead of throwing his hands up and giving up, George has instead triumphed. His persistence is a challenge to others to not take the easy route but to get involved and address this issue of misperception.

Rating: Quote Machine

> **"It's about raising awareness of these issues and breaking down perceptions."**

Here George is referring to divide between rich and poor and the income inequality that exists in this country. This inequality leads to the increased likelihood of inner-city and low-income youth becoming involved in crime or violence and a higher rate of teen pregnancy. He knows that the way to deal with the problems that many youths face is by first overcoming the basic prejudices and **stereotypes** people have. This is done through raising awareness of the situation of these youths. Through this awareness, a more thoughtful approach can be taken to address their problems and help these youths see themselves in a more positive light.

Rating: Quote Machine

George works to break down the stereotype of inner-city kids being prone to crime and violence.

George took an Indiana Pacers team that had not been accustomed to winning and helped them see that a change in attitude was needed for them to compete with the best teams in the league. His efforts led the team to back-to-back Eastern Conference finals. In fact, during his time in Indiana, the team finished no worse than third place in their division, except for the 2014–2015 season, which he missed due to injury. George has grown so used to winning that he seeks to surround himself with those teammates who share his commitment to excellence. The way he sees things, second place is simply the first loser—he would prefer to be around people with a winning mentality and not a losing one.

"If you ain't got a mind-set to win, if you're happy being second, I can't deal with you."

Rating: Quote Machine

"I've never played the game with any hesitancy. That's the reason I'm probably in this cast. I play my hardest, I give my all, I leave it all on the floor. Not one moment do I expect to get injured or feel limited on the court. Although I'm not looking at that right now, I won't be hesitant when I come back."

Most players when selected to represent the country as a part of Team USA, or selected to an All-Star game, tend to give half the effort they would normally give. An injury could have a tremendous impact on their career and future earning potential. This often results in contests that are not interesting to watch. George, in this quote, explains that he plays the game

Whether playing against average players or NBA superstar LeBron James, George gives his best effort every time he steps on the court.

hard all the time, regardless of the situation, whether practice, a game, an exhibition, or the NBA All-Star game. This attitude is a healthy one to see in a player of his status in the league, even if it cost him nearly all of the 2014 season because of an injury he suffered in a seemingly meaningless exhibition. Based on the numbers he has put up since coming back, it doesn't appear that the injury has held him back. **Rating: Quote Machine**

STRENGTH FROM INJURY

Up until the 2014–2015 NBA season, George had not experienced any significant breaks or injuries. This changed just before the start of the 2014 season. Working out with Team USA in preparation for the World Cup of Basketball Championships, he suffered an unfortunate lower leg injury. The injury was serious enough to keep him from making the team, which went on to win the gold medal in Barcelona, Spain. The injury could have been serious enough to prevent him from ever playing again; fortunately, he was able to recover and resume his career without missing a beat.

He is seen using crutches as he addresses the media on the nature of a leg injury he suffered at the start of the 2014–2015 NBA season, which kept him sidelined for 76 of the season's 82 games.

This quote relates to the terrible injury he suffered in 2014 but is not limited to it. George has experienced the triumph of victory in the NBA and seen his teams advance far in the playoffs. He has also been on the receiving end of crushing defeat and been left to wonder what's next. George knows that experiencing the worst thing, whether it's a leg break or a loss in game 6 of the 2014 Eastern Conference finals, only leads to you experiencing the best thing that happens next that much more intensely. This attitude certainly helped lead him to new opportunities for winning in Oklahoma City and then Los Angeles. **Rating: Quote Machine**

> "There are two sides to everything. The worst has happened. The best is next."

> "Don't tell me the sky is the limit when there are footprints on the moon"

This is a quote from George that gives insight into how he views what he believes is the limit to potential. He is a firm believer that we can all reach even higher than we believed possible. It is a definite cliché, but pushing our limits to only the sky, to him, seems shortsighted. He believes that the once you reach the sky, you should push further to the moon. He probably believes that reaching the moon should not stop you from pushing even further in the universe, maybe toward the sun or wherever represents the highest of heights. **Rating: Cliché City**

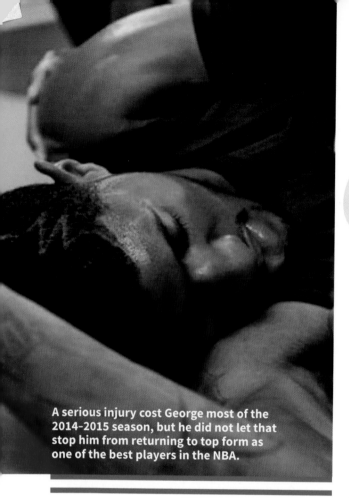

A serious injury cost George most of the 2014–2015 season, but he did not let that stop him from returning to top form as one of the best players in the NBA.

> ## "Never let defeat have the last word."

George never played in a postseason game during his two seasons at Fresno State University. The teams that he played on were not very good, but George was able to make the best of a bad situation to raise his profile and eventually become a top-10 pick in 2010. George worked hard in his first couple of seasons in Indiana, including obtaining a Most Improved Player award while improving his game to help turn things around for the Pacers and make them a top team in the league's Eastern Conference. This old Tibetan proverb is a favorite quote of George's. His work ethic and dedication to winning drives George to continue to improve and surround himself with people with the same commitment to winning. Where most people will suffer defeats for a long time, George refuses to accept losing as any kind of final say on his eventual success. **Rating: Cliché City**

> **"Getting people into the wilderness for a transcendent experience empowers people for years, if not for their entire lives."**

George is a person who believes in communing with nature. He finds that spending time in nature provides a way for people to gain a different perspective on life. This makes sense considering where George was raised. He grew up in the mountain valley community of Palmdale, California. This city is far from the hustle and bustle of Los Angeles and it was a place that allowed him to distance himself from the types of things other kids his age went through, such as drugs and violence. George believes that spending time in nature is something everyone should do, if for no other reason than to recharge his or her batteries and gain new insight. **Rating: Quote Machine**

George grew up in the Los Angeles suburb of Palmdale.

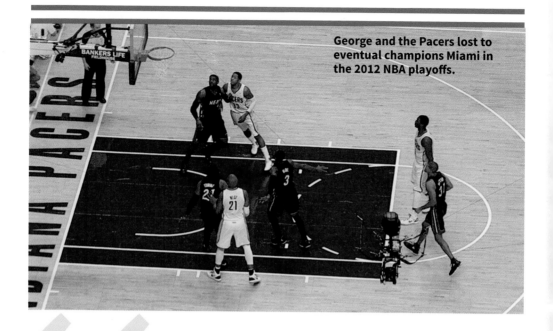

George and the Pacers lost to eventual champions Miami in the 2012 NBA playoffs.

"We came out to win and knew that we were going to battle back and win game 4 and game 5. We were all fired up, and the emotional level of wanting it more allowed us to come out on top."

George and the Indiana Pacers suffered a 4–2 series loss against the Miami Heat in 2012. The team his Pacers faced featured the trio of LeBron James, Dwyane Wade, and Chris Bosh, all soon-to-be members of basketball's Hall of Fame. After the Heat went up three games to one, George dropped 37 points on Miami, grabbed six boards, and stole the ball six times from the Heat in a 93–90 game 5 victory. Although they lost in game 6 to the eventual NBA champions, this quote talks about the mind-set the team had going into the game, which drove it to victory in game 5. **Rating: Quote Machine**

TEXT-DEPENDENT QUESTIONS

1. In what year was George's season shortened due to an injury? What part of his body was injured?

2. How many games did he play in his injury-shortened season?

3. How many seasons (number) did the Indiana Pacers appear in the Eastern Conference Finals during the time he played for the team?

RESEARCH PROJECT

George injured himself prior to the start of the 2014 season, but was able to come back and return to his all-star form. He has been named to the NBA All-Star team (for both the Eastern and Western Conference) six times in his career. George was named to four of those squads after suffering his injury. Looking back at the league for the period 2001–2018, find three other players who suffered a serious injury that caused them to miss an entire NBA season. List the team that these players were on at the time of the injury, the nature of the injury, the season they returned to the league (and with what team if different), and the number of All-Star teams they were named to after their injuries.

WORDS TO UNDERSTAND

circuit: An association of similar groups; league

existential: Grounded in existence or the experience of existence

Zen: A state of calm attentiveness in which one's actions are guided by intuition rather than by conscious effort

CHAPTER 5

OFF THE COURT
GEORGE'S EDUCATION

George graduated from high school in 2008 and went on to attend college at California State University at Fresno in the fall. He played two years for the Bulldogs' men's basketball team and eventually entered the NBA draft after his sophomore year. George has done well for himself since joining the league but has not yet earned his degree from Fresno State or any other school.

George's older sisters attended college and played college sports as well. His oldest sister Portala attended California State University at San Bernardino where she played volleyball, while his other sister Teiosha was a small forward at Pepperdine University. Both sisters graduated from their respective schools, raising the prospect that at some point the pressure of his older siblings' academic accomplishments may force George to return to campus for his degree.

GEORGE AT HOME

George signed his rookie deal with the Indiana Pacers in 2010 for a reported $10.5 million (see "Salary Information" section below). With his newfound wealth, George purchased a home in Indianapolis for $2.2 million. The home featured five bedrooms, eight separate bathrooms, and 12,605 square feet of space (1,171 sq. m). The house has 360-degree views of its own private lake. The estate was certainly fitting of his status as a rising NBA star, but when George accepted a trade to Oklahoma City, it was time to give up his luxurious house and move to his other home in California. George placed his Indianapolis home on the market for sale in 2017, after inking his four-year $134 million deal with the Thunder; it was listed on the real estate website Zillow for $2.1 million, which is $100,000 less than he paid for it.

George's house in Indiana was on a private lake.

George is now a residence in the Los Angeles–area community of Chatsworth, California. His California home is 5,336 square feet (496 sq. m), which he purchased in 2012 for the price of $1.5 million. For a single man with no dependents, George requires a lot of space in a home. Whether it's due to his six-foot-nine-inch (2.09 m) frame or his need for room, he has the perfect home to meet his needs!

GEORGE'S CAR COLLECTION

George has a love of powerful automobiles. Playing in the NBA has afforded him the chance to invest in an impressive car collection. George began the collection when he signed his rookie deal with Indiana and has added such vehicles as the Porsche Panamera and Ferrari 458 Italia. For perspective, the costs of these two cars are as follows:

- Porsche Panamera, MSRP* $88,500–$99,600 (depending on the vehicle model)
- Ferrari 458 Italia, MSRP $237,600

*MSRP—Manufacturer's Suggested Retail Price

The Ferrari 458 Italia, which George purchased in 2014, was the envy of his teammates and other players in the league. He paid $370,000 for his customized model designed for his six-foot-nine-inch frame, making it the most valuable asset in George's luxury car collection. If you need a car that goes from zero to 60 miles per hour (zero to 96.56 kilometers per hour) in 3.4 seconds (and you probably don't), $230,000 to $370,000 in your wallet will get you this car!

George's also has a Ferrari F430 ($187,925 to $308,000 MSRP) and a Jeep Wrangler ($23,995 to $39,145 MSRP), giving his collection a retail value of more than a million dollars. He has been fortunate that his basketball talent has made it possible to fund his love for expensive cars.

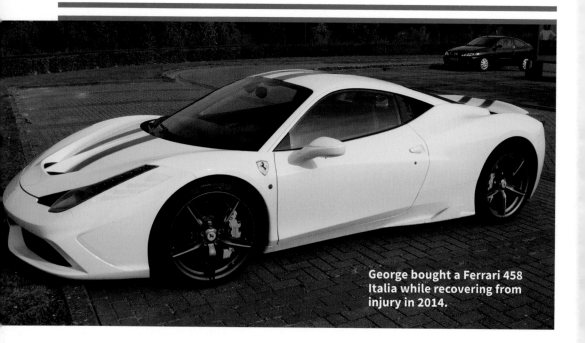

George bought a Ferrari 458 Italia while recovering from injury in 2014.

GIVING BACK TO THE COMMUNITY

George is very involved with the community in whichever city he is living. Whether that was something he learned as a young boy growing up or something he developed over time as he became more successful as an NBA player, there is a sense that his charitable nature is a genuine extension of who George is as a person. He has created the Paul George Foundation, an organization committed to providing funding to a variety of different causes. He supports efforts that help youth gain access to technology (i.e., computers), improve schools, and promote outdoor activities. One of the activities that George is passionate about is fishing. He has sponsored opportunities for area youth in Oklahoma City to go on fishing trips with him as a way to allow them to experience life in the outdoors.

GEORGE THE FISHERMAN

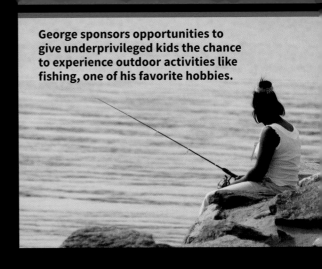

George sponsors opportunities to give underprivileged kids the chance to experience outdoor activities like fishing, one of his favorite hobbies.

One of George's favorite hobbies is fishing. It is something that he has enjoyed since childhood and is a passion that has carried on into his adult life. Fishing is a **Zen**-inducing hobby that allows him to get away from the pressures of needing to win on the court and focus on becoming one with himself (his **existential** being). He has participated in fishing tournaments as an adult and also has used his foundation as a platform for connecting youth with the outdoors. Perhaps, once he has finished his NBA career and has hung up his shoes, you might find him on the bass fishing **circuit**.

AMERICAN STROKE ASSOCIATION

George's mother Paulette suffered a stroke when he was six years old. The stroke was of a serious enough nature that it kept her bedridden for about two years. Seeing his mother bedbound and unable to care for herself deeply affected George, so when he had the opportunity, he decided to support the American Stroke Association (ASA), an organization that works on behalf of stroke sufferers.

The ASA is a national charitable association based in Dallas, Texas. The organization is a division of the American Heart Association and is focused on

Fishing is an activity that George promotes through his foundation. It is an opportunity to take youths that would normally not be on the water and expose them to an experience different from their everyday life.

providing education, support, and a voice for those sufferers of strokes in the United States. According to the Centers for Disease Control located in Atlanta, Georgia, nearly 800,000 people in the country suffer from some type of stroke each year.

George's mother Paulette recovered from her stroke, but the experience led to George dedicating his time and resources toward educating people about the health risks leading to strokes. He has teamed up with the American Stroke Association, appearing in public service announcements and raising money to help the organization with its outreach efforts.

MARKETING GEORGE

George has endorsement deals with the following products:

- Gatorade
- Infinity Ward
- *Call of Duty* (video game)
- Jeep
- New Era
- Nike

George is represented by Aaron Mintz, an agent associated with Creative Artists Agency. Mintz is listed number 37 on Forbes list of top-earning sports agents, with $470.4 million in contracts negotiated

The Centers for Disease Control is a federal agency tasked with preventing the spread of disease and using research and education to warn about the risk factors for things like heart attack or stroke.

among his 20 clients (George's $134 million contract represents a little less than a third of this amount). The contract George received from Oklahoma City in his 2017 trade was the maximum allowed under the new collective bargain agreement between the league and the players association.

SALARY INFORMATION

George signed his first contract as a rookie in 2010, which was a four-year deal worth $10.5 million with the Indiana Pacers. He signed a five-year veteran's contract in 2014 valued $91.6 million, which would have kept George in an Indiana Pacers uniform through the end of the 2018–2019 season. He passed on the final year of the deal (worth $20.7 million) and accepted a four-year, $136.9 million guaranteed free agent contract with the Oklahoma City Thunder.

Here is a breakdown of his salary earnings since his rookie season in 2010:

Season	Team	Salary
2010–11	Indiana Pacers	$ 2,238,360
2011–12	Indiana Pacers	$ 2,406,240
2012–13	Indiana Pacers	$ 2,574,120

Season	Team	Salary
2013–14	Indiana Pacers	$ 3,282,003
2014–15	Indiana Pacers	$ 15,925,680
2015–16	Indiana Pacers	$ 17,120,106
2016–17	Indiana Pacers	$ 18,314,532
2017–18	Oklahoma City Thunder	$ 19,508,958
2018–19	Oklahoma City Thunder	$ 30,560,700
2019–20	Los Angeles Clippers	$ 33,005,556
2020–21	Los Angeles Clippers	$ 35,450,412
2021–22	Los Angeles Clippers	$ 37,895,268
TOTAL		**$238,985,319**

Paul, here decked out in Nike gear for the national team at the 2016 Olympics, played his last season in Indiana following the Rio games.

George has reached the top of his profession and is regarded as one of the best players at his position. Starting from very humble beginnings when he wasn't even viewed as the best player in his state coming out of high school, George has become a consistent three-point threat, ball thief, and player with the ability to take over a game in order to impose his will to win. He is striving to be considered not just a good small forward in the NBA but one of the greatest and most complete players at his, or any, position.

George's first nine seasons showed the league that he is ready to take his place among the NBA's best. Only time will tell whether his commitment to becoming the best player will result in his being a player we will remember long after his shoes are hanging in the Pro Basketball Hall of Fame in Springfield, Massachusetts.

TEXT-DEPENDENT QUESTIONS

1. What organization did George create to fund various causes?

2. What was the total value of his rookie contract? What amount would he have received from Indiana if he had stayed for his 2018–2019 season?

3. What is George's favorite hobby?

RESEARCH PROJECT

For many players, having a hobby outside of the game of basketball is a great release from the pressures of having to perform at a high level. Having some interest that is different from basketball allows a player to develop into a more well-rounded and complete person. For George, his go-to hobby in the off-season is fishing. Looking at the top-10 draft selections from each of the last 10 NBA drafts (2009–2018), do research to see what the hobbies are of each of the players drafted in those positions (total 100 players). For those still active in the NBA as of the 2018–2019 season, describe the activity and how different the activity is from playing for an NBA team.

SERIES GLOSSARY OF KEY TERMS

assist: a pass that directly leads to a teammate making a basket.

blocked shot: when a defensive player stops a shot at the basket by hitting the ball away.

center: a player whose main job is to score near the basket and win offensive and defensive rebounds. Centers are usually the tallest players on the court, and the best are able to move with speed and agility.

double dribble: when a player dribbles the ball with two hands or stops dribbling and starts again. The opposing team gets the ball.

field goal: a successful shot worth two points—three points if shot from behind the three-point line.

foul: called by the officials for breaking a rule: reaching in, blocking, charging, and over the back, for example. If a player commits six fouls during the game, he fouls out and must leave play. If an offensive player is fouled while shooting, he usually gets two foul shots (one shot if the player's basket counted or three if he was fouled beyond the three-point line).

foul shot: a "free throw," an uncontested shot taken from the foul line (15 feet [4.6 m]) from the basket.

goaltending: when a defensive player touches the ball after it has reached its highest point on the way to the basket. The team on offense gets the points they would have received from the basket. Goaltending is also called on any player, on offense or defense, who slaps the backboard or touches the ball directly above the basket.

jump ball: when an official puts the ball into play by tossing it in the air. Two opposing players try to tip it to their own teammate.

man-to-man defense: when each defensive player guards a single offensive player.

officials: those who monitor the action and call fouls. In the NBA there are three for each game.

point guard: the player who handles the ball most on offense. He brings the ball up the court and tries to create scoring opportunities through passing. Good point guards are quick, good passers, and can see the court well.

power forward: a player whose main jobs are to score from close to the basket and win offensive and defensive rebounds. Good power forwards are tall and strong.

rebound: when a player gains possession of the ball after a missed shot.

roster: the players on a team. NBA teams have 12-player rosters.

shooting guard: a player whose main job is to score using jump shots and drives to the basket. Good shooting guards are usually taller than point guards but still quick.

shot clock: a 24-second clock that starts counting down when a team gets the ball. The clock restarts whenever the ball changes possession. If the offense does not shoot the ball in time, it turns the ball over to the other team.

small forward: a player whose main job is to score from inside or outside. Good small forwards are taller than point or shooting guards and have speed and agility.

steal: when a defender takes the ball from an opposing player.

technical foul: called by the official for misconduct or a procedural violation. The team that does not commit the foul gets possession of the ball and a free throw.

three-point play: a two-point field goal combined with a successful free throw. This happens when an offensive player makes a basket but is fouled in the process.

three-point shot: a field goal made from behind the three-point line.

traveling: when a player moves, taking three steps or more, without dribbling, also called "walking." The opposing team gets the ball.

turnover: when the offensive team loses the ball: passing the ball out of bounds, traveling, or double dribbling, for example.

zone defense: when each defensive player guards within a specific area of the court. Common zones include 2-1-2, 1-3-1, or 2-3. Zone defense has only recently been allowed in the NBA.

FURTHER READING

Goodman, Michael E. *Oklahoma City Thunder*. Mankato, MN: The Creative Company, 2018.

Grange, Michael. *Basketball's Greatest Stars*. Richmond Hills, ON: Firefly Books, Limited, 2018.

MacMullan, Jackie, Rafe Bartholomew, and Dan Klores. *Basketball: A Love Story*. New York: Crown Archetype, 2018.

Serrano, Shea. *Basketball (and Other Things): A Collection of Questions Asked, Answered, Illustrated*. New York: Abrams Books, 2017.

Whiting, Jim. *The NBA: A History of Hoops: Indiana Pacers*. Mankato, MN: The Creative Company, 2017.

INTERNET RESOURCES

https://www.basketball-reference.com/players/g/georgpa01.html
The basketball-specific resource provided by Sports Reference LLC for current and historical statistics of Paul George.

http://bleacherreport.com/nba
The official website for Bleacher Report Sport's NBA reports on each of the 30 teams.

https://www.cbssports.com/nba/teams/OKC/oklahoma-city-thunder/
The web page for the Oklahoma City Thunder provided by CBSSports.com, providing latest news and information, player profiles, scheduling, and standings.

https://newsok.com/sports/thunder
The web page of *The Oklahoman* (Oklahoma City) newspaper for the Oklahoma City Thunder basketball team.

www.espn.com/nba/team/_/name/okc/oklahoma-city-thunder
The official website of ESPN sports network for the Oklahoma City Thunder.

http://www.nba.com/#/
The official website of the National Basketball Association.

https://www.nba.com/thunder/
The official NBA website for the Oklahoma City Thunder basketball team, including history, player information, statistics, and news.

https://sports.yahoo.com/nba/
The official website of Yahoo! Sports NBA coverage, providing news, statistics, and important information about the association and its 30 teams.

INDEX

INDEX

INDEX

EDUCATIONAL VIDEO LINKS

Pg. 12: http://x-qr.net/1KSm

Pg. 13: http://x-qr.net/1KkG

Pg. 14: http://x-qr.net/1Hye

Pg. 15: http://x-qr.net/1Lcu

Pg. 16: http://x-qr.net/1JnX

Pg. 17: http://x-qr.net/1JBW

Pg. 18: http://x-qr.net/1LL0

Pg. 19: http://x-qr.net/1JKe

Pg. 32: http://x-qr.net/1KDc

Pg. 48: http://x-qr.net/1KJT

Pg. 58: http://x-qr.net/1K0K

Pg. 70: http://x-qr.net/1KbA

PHOTO CREDITS

AUTHOR BIOGRAPHY

Donald Parker is an avid sports fan, author, and father. He enjoys watching and participating in many types of sports, including football, basketball, baseball, and golf. He enjoyed a brief career as a punter and defensive back at NCAA Division III Carroll College (now University) in Waukesha, Wisconsin, and spends much of his time now watching and writing about the sports he loves.